• • THE LIBRARY OF FAMOUS WOMEN • •

ANNE FRANK

Child of the Holocaust

by
Gene Brown

A BLACKBIRCH PRESS BOOK

WOODBRIDGE, CONNECTICUT

Published by Blackbirch Press, Inc.
One Bradley Road
Woodbridge, CT 06525

©1991 Blackbirch Press, Inc.
First Edition

Printed in Hong Kong

10 9 8 7 6 5 4 3 2

Library of Congress Cataloging-in-Publication Data

Brown, Gene.
    Anne Frank: child of the holocaust/Gene Brown
      p.   cm. — (The Library of famous women)
    Includes bibliographical references and index.
    Summary: A biography of the thirteen-year-old Jewish girl whose diary, published after her death in a Nazi concentration camp, made her famous all over the world.
    ISBN 1-56711-030-4   ISBN 1-56711-049-5 (softcover)
    1. Frank, Anne, 1929–1945—Juvenile literature. 2. Jews—Netherlands—Amsterdam—Biography—Juvenile literature. 3. Holocaust, Jewish (1939–1945)—Netherlands—Amsterdam—Biography—Juvenile literature. 4. Amsterdam (Netherlands)—Biography—Juvenile literature. [1. Frank, Anne, 1929–1945. 2. Jews—Biography. 3. Holocaust, Jewish (1939–1945)] I. Title. II. Series.
DS135.N6F732 1991
940.53'18'092—dc20
[B]

                                     91-13702
                                        CIP
                                        AC

Contents

Introduction

Why would anyone want to read about the most private thoughts of a 13-year-old girl? That's what Anne Frank asked herself as she wrote in her diary in the early 1940s. She was, after all, an ordinary 13-year-old. Her parents didn't seem to understand her. She often couldn't figure out the boys she knew. And she did not care for some of her teachers.

Anne wasn't even known as a good writer. One of her teachers said that "the compositions that Anne wrote in school were just ordinary, no better than average."

Yet millions of people have read Anne's diary and seen the play and movie based on it. Most were deeply moved. The diary has been translated into many languages, and Anne Frank's name is known all over the world. The place in the Netherlands where she wrote her famous diary is now a museum.

Anne is famous because she was able to write about a subject for which the world's best writers have been unable to find the right words. She was one of 6 million Jews murdered by the Nazis during World War II. She died in what we now call the "Holocaust." (The word means a great fire, often used to burn a sacrifice.) Her diary tells of how she and her family hid from the Nazis and tried to keep a little hope alive when much of the world seemed to be going mad.

The room in the Annex, where Anne and her family hid, is today part of a museum collection housed in that same building.

Chapter 1

Flight from Evil

Anne Frank was born in Germany, the country in which the Nazis came to power. Jews had lived in Germany for hundreds of years. Often they were victims of prejudice, much like that faced by some groups, such as blacks in the United States.

Anne, in her yearly portrait, taken in May 1935.

The family of Otto Frank, Anne's father, had lived in Frankfurt, Germany, for a long time. About 30 thousand Jews lived there—5 percent of the city's people. Only Berlin, the capital, had more Jews than Frankfurt. There was anti-Jewish feeling in Anne's hometown. For example, some restaurants refused to serve Jews. Yet compared with the rest of Germany, Frankfurt was tolerant. Otto could recall no *anti-Semitic* (anti-Jewish) incidents when he was growing up. By the early 1930s, the city even had a Jewish mayor.

(Opposite page) Children play outside the house in Frankfurt, Germany, where Anne was born.

Otto and Edith Frank

Otto's family did well in the retail department store business and he decided to make it his career too. In 1908, Otto dropped out of college and spent a year in New York, working in Macy's department store. The parents of a friend he had met at school owned the store.

Like other young men his age, Otto served in the German army during World War I. He joined in 1915, became an officer, and won several medals. After the war, he went into business for himself.

In 1925, Otto married Edith Hollander, whose family was also in business. Their first daughter, Margot, was born the next year. Anne was born in 1929.

In that year, the Great Depression began to spread through the United States and Europe. Stores closed, businesses failed, and many people lost their jobs. One out of every four persons in Frankfurt was unemployed. Those still working worried that they might be the next to become jobless.

Hard times made it easier for the Nazis and Adolf Hitler, their leader, to gain support. Many Germans were frightened. They were ready to believe anyone who promised them a better and more secure life. Hitler told them that Germany didn't need freedom. It needed a leader to tell the country's people what to do—someone they should obey without question. He said he was that leader.

Hitler also played on German prejudices. He placed the blame for everything that had gone wrong in their country on the Jews and on other people who were unpopular. These included gypsies, homosexuals, communists, and anyone who looked, thought, or acted differently from other Germans. Get rid of these "outsiders," he said, and Germany's problems would go away. Soon, Hitler organized a movement headed by his own Nazi Party.

The Nazis Take Control

In 1933, when Anne was four years old, the Nazis had almost complete power in Germany. The Franks watched with increasing alarm what the Nazis did. The Nazis quickly moved against their "enemies." When they found books with ideas they didn't like, they burned them. The Nazis also built concentration camps— large prisons—for those who opposed them. At first, people sent to these camps simply lost their freedom. Later, the concentration camps would become scenes of torture and mass killing.

Anne (left) and older sister Margot, around 1933.

Adolph Hitler rides through Nuremberg, Germany, in 1938, waving to Nazi supporters as he passes.

Jews got the worst treatment in Germany. They could no longer hold government jobs. All Jewish officials, like the mayor of Frankfurt, had to resign. Non-Jewish Germans were ordered not to go to Jewish doctors or hire Jewish lawyers. In the schools, Jewish students were segregated— put in separate classes. Jewish teachers were fired. Jews who owned stores had to mark their windows with the word "Jew." Before long, the Nazis forced Jews to sell their businesses to non-Jews. These rules affected anyone who had even one Jewish grandparent.

Few Germans spoke out against these new rules. Many believed Hitler's lies about the Jews. Those who didn't were afraid of being sent to a concentration camp if they said what they thought. Even the Catholic and Protestant churches did little to stop the Nazis.

The Nazis used the gestapo—their secret police—to scare people. The gestapo was brutal and had spies everywhere. The Nazis also frightened people with their storm troopers—party members who dressed like soldiers and acted like thugs. They began to beat Jews in the street.

Otto decided not to wait. He feared that conditions in Germany would get worse. Otto made up his mind to get his family out of the country. He sent Edith and his daughters to live in the German city of Aachen, where his wife's family lived. Meanwhile, he got a job working for a company in Amsterdam, Holland, in the Netherlands, a country bordering Germany. About 90,000 Jews lived in Amsterdam. From there, Otto sent for his family.

Why did Otto Frank choose the Netherlands? It was close to home and, in many ways, like the area from which his family came. Jews had been treated fairly well there for many centuries, making Otto think it would be a safe place. He could not have been more wrong.

Thousands of Hitler youth gather in the city of Berchtesgaden in April, 1935, to celebrate Hitler's birthday.

Chapter 2

Another Escape

Anne Frank grew up when terrible things were beginning to happen in the world. But her parents could still give her and Margot a loving and secure family life. Anne had good memories of her early years. For example, she could recall many of her parents' friends coming to visit on Sundays, and the wonderful smell of the coffee and cake that was served.

Anne was a slim girl with dark brown hair, intense dark eyes, and dimples. Visitors to the Frank home were likely to be greeted by the sight of her carrying her cat, Moortje. The cat's hind legs almost touched the floor as little Anne struggled to hold him.

Anne's sister, Margot, got better grades in school and was the more serious of the two. Anne called her "brainy." Margot was well-behaved and kept her clothes and other things neat. Anne was messier with her belongings. She also had high spirits.

People remembered her strong personality, which sometimes got her in trouble at school.

Margot was quiet and thoughtful, while Anne liked to say whatever was on her mind. This trait could be refreshing and honest, although at times some people found it thoughtless. Once, Anne told one of her parents' friends that his eyes were like a cat's. The friend found that very funny. But the other adults in the room considered it impolite for Anne to talk that way to an adult.

Anne liked attention, and she often got it by making people laugh. When she was only four years old, her mother wrote to a friend that Anne was like "a little comedian." Later, Anne loved to perform in school plays. She also enjoyed doing imitations—whether of a friend, a teacher, or even a cat.

By the time she was in grade school, Anne had many friends. Anne and her friends like to play pingpong and a game similar to hopscotch. They also did handstands against the wall in a nearby playground. Anne was a bit clumsy, though, and sometimes fell over. No matter what Anne and her friends played, they usually went out for ice cream after the game.

Margot Frank poses in front of her school in 1936, age 10.

The mother of a friend of Anne's once said that, even when young, Anne seemed to "know who she was." She meant that Anne had a good sense of herself, that she was mature for her age. Yet Anne could also be childish. Sometimes she swung from one way of behaving to the other: an adult one minute, a child the next.

Anne had strong opinions about the people she knew. She thought that some of the other students in her school were "absolute cuckoos," and that a few of her teachers were "freaks." Her math teacher thought that she talked too much in class. To punish her, he made her write a composition about why she couldn't be quiet. That didn't silence her, so he next told her to write about what her constant talking reminded him of: "quack, quack, quack." She won him over by writing, instead, a funny poem about talking.

At age 11, most girls her age were still playing children's games. Anne and her friends, however, were already "giggling over the boys," according to one girl who knew her. Anne was very aware of her effect on the boys around her. They constantly flirted with her.

As she approached her teenage years, Anne became very interested in how she

Anne at her desk in primary school.

looked. She and her friends often read fashion magazines. They thought of her as "stylish."

One day, a girl who knew Anne was at the local dressmaker's shop with her mother. The dressmaker was in the fitting room with a customer. "It would look better with larger shoulder pads," they heard the customer say behind the curtain, "and the hemline should be just a little higher, don't you think?" The girl was surprised when the curtains parted and out came Anne Frank. She was the person who seemed to have known just what she wanted, sounding, for a moment, like an adult.

In ordinary times, Anne might have looked forward to being a teenager much like any other girl. But these were not ordinary times. Conditions kept getting worse in Germany throughout the 1930s, especially for the Jews. Before long, the Nazis were threatening to bring their system of hate, fear, and terror to other countries around the world.

Life in Germany Grows Worse

In 1935, Germany took all political rights away from its Jewish citizens. It was as if they were no longer Germans, but foreigners in their own country. Jews could no longer marry non-Jews. Many Jews, fearing for their lives, left Germany. These people had to leave behind most of their property.

In 1938, all Jewish students were ordered out of German schools. At the end of that year, the Nazis staged mass arrests of Jews, sending 30,000 to concentration camps. They also encouraged mobs to attack Jews throughout the country—in their homes, shops, and synagogues. One hundred Jews were killed as the mobs left a path of destruction—200 synagogues and 5,000 stores were destroyed. There was so much broken glass afterwards on the streets that the attack became known as "Crystal Night," although the violence lasted several days.

The Nazis forced Jews to wear a yellow Star of David on the outside of their clothing. In this way, Jews could be easily recognized. This meant that there was almost no place in Germany where Jews could be safe.

People all over the world were horrified. There were complaints to the German government, but they did no good. Many Jews remaining in Germany now tried to get out. Two of Anne Frank's aunts left for the United States. Anne's grandmother left Aachen and went to Amsterdam to live

In November, 1938, Nazis set fire to the Fasanenstrasse Synagogue. The synagogue was the largest house of Jewish worship in the city of Berlin.

with Anne's family. By 1939, half the Jews who had lived in Germany had left.

Most of the Jews still living in Germany could have been saved, but many couldn't leave. They had nowhere to go. Other countries, including the Netherlands and the United States, only took in a certain number of new people from other nations. They might bend the rules a little for those who were in danger, like the German Jews, but not much.

The countries that Jews wanted to move to said that they were worried about not having enough jobs for all the newcomers. Or they said they didn't have enough housing—any number of reasons were given. Often the reasons had more to do with prejudice. Jews weren't wanted because they were Jews. Anti-Semitism was everywhere, not just in Germany.

A young Berlin man clears broken glass from shattered shop windows, destroyed during "Crystal Night" on November 9, 1938. Thousands of Jewish shops were looted and demolished by Nazis who wanted Jews out of Germany.

17

Anne wrote this letter to an American pen-pal just days before the Germans invaded the Netherlands. The letter tells of Anne's everyday life and asks for the address of additional pen-pals.

Throughout the 1930s, the Nazis said that Germans needed more "room to live." In 1939, when Anne was 10, Hitler took direct action to obtain more land. His armies invaded Poland. Great Britain and France came to Poland's defense. When they declared war on Germany, they officially began World War II.

At first, the war did not touch the Dutch, as the people of the Netherlands were called. Until 1940, the Netherlands seemed a safe place for Jews—compared to much of the rest of Europe.

There were 140,000 Jews living in the Netherlands. About 24,000 of them had fled from Germany. There was anti-Semitism, but the Franks encountered little of it. That's why Anne could lead a fairly normal life.

Amsterdam Becomes Dangerous

On May 10, 1940, the hopes for a peaceful life in their new country were dashed. Otto Frank was at his office that day and his face turned pale as he heard the report on the radio: the Germans had attacked the Netherlands. The Dutch fought back, but they were quickly beaten. It was over in four days.

A deep shadow was suddenly cast over Anne's life—and over that of everyone she knew. The Germans used the Dutch Nazi party to help them rule the Netherlands. Gradually, the new government began to repeat what was happening in Germany.

Jews could not teach or work for the Dutch government. They couldn't go to public places like movies and libraries. Dutch Nazis began to attack Jews on the street. They also began to arrest some Jews and send them to concentration camps. Soon the Nazis were regularly arresting large numbers of Jews on the street and taking them to prison.

Beginning in 1942, Jews, including children like Anne, had to wear a yellow Star of David on the left side of their coat. They had to wear the star even when they came to open their front door. When many non-Jews began to wear it in sympathy, the Germans arrested them. Dutch workers also protested the treatment of the Jews by going out on strike. The Nazis broke the strike after a few days.

Jews weren't allowed to go anywhere with their non-Jewish Dutch friends. They also had a curfew: they had to be indoors by 8:00 at night.

By 1942, Jews in Germany were required to wear a yellow Star of David on their clothing so others could plainly see their religion.

It was hard enough being young and dealing with the usual criticism a child expects from her parents. Now Anne's mother and father had very real reasons to be concerned for her safety. One night, Anne was walking with a boy and came in a few minutes after eight, making her father very angry. She wasn't used to such toughness from him, and he didn't like being so cross with her. But he knew she could have been arrested.

A Wonderful Birthday Present

In the middle of this tense time, on June 12th, 1942, Anne turned 13. Her father's birthday present to her was a diary—a book with blank pages and a red-checkered hard cover. In it she could write about what happened in her life each day. She also could record her thoughts and feelings about anything or anybody.

In her first entry in the diary, Anne gave the book a name: "Kitty." She wrote that she and the diary would be "pals." Anne felt that she needed a friend with whom she could share her serious thoughts, and the diary would be it. She couldn't really do that with any of her family or friends. Kitty, unlike others in her life, would always be patient and willing to listen.

Anne's diary

A wounded man peers at a dead child, lying on a street in Amsterdam, Holland. The child was killed during the Nazi invasion of May, 1940.

It would have been hard for Anne to write only about personal things in her diary. Too many horrible events were happening in the outside world. The Nazis were rounding up Jews as if they were animals. One Dutch woman passing a home for Jewish orphans said she saw "the Germans were loading the children, who ranged in ages from babies to eight-year-olds, on trucks. When they did not move fast enough the Nazis picked them up, by an arm, a leg, the hair, and threw them into the trucks."

What were Jews like the Franks to do? Everyone had to have an identification card. Besides, most Dutch had blond hair and blue eyes. Jews, like Anne, were likely to have dark hair and dark eyes. Their appearance made them stand out.

As a result, many Jews went into hiding. They found Dutch non-Jews who had attics, basements, or extra rooms in which they could stay. The Dutch who hid Jews faced arrest if they were found out.

No Place to Run

By the beginning of the summer of 1942, Anne's parents were thinking of hiding themselves and their children from the Nazis. They began to move some of their belongings to the houses of non-Jewish friends, who would keep them safe until after the war. On July 5, Otto told Anne that they might have to hide.

That afternoon, the Franks sped up their plan. Margot received a notice requiring that she report for forced labor in Germany. The Nazis used many young people, including Dutch non-Jews, to do work that had been done by Germans now serving in the army. If 16-year-old Margot didn't report, she would be arrested. If she did go, the Germans would make her a slave.

That settled it. Otto had already picked out a hiding place. It was the rooms used for storage, called the "Annex," above the office he managed. He had talked to one of his workers, a Dutch woman named Miep Gies, about helping him and his family remain safe there. She agreed to help. She told a few other workers at the office who promised to keep the Frank's hiding place a secret. They also would bring the family food and anything else they needed until the war ended.

A young Miep Gies poses for a photograph. Through Miep's great efforts, the Frank family was able to hide safely from the Nazis for two years.

The Franks were to be joined in their hiding place by another Jewish family, Mr. van Daan and his wife and son. Mr. van Daan worked with Otto Frank.

Margot was in the most danger, so she went to the hiding place immediately. Anne and her parents soon followed. (Anne's grandmother had died by this time.) The van Daans came a week later.

Anne did not have much time to get ready, and she couldn't carry many of her belongings to the Annex because it would look suspicious. She put just a few items in her school bag. The first thing she packed was her diary. It was a warm, rainy Monday morning, but Anne wore several layers of clothing to sneak clothes into the hideout without drawing attention.

Anne could not say goodbye to her friends because the family's secret might have gotten out. Once safe in the hiding place, Anne wrote a letter to one of her pals explaining what had happened, but it was never mailed.

Otto Frank said that he and his family were "disappearing." Anne thought of it as a "vacation." Later, she would call it an "adventure." As Miep Gies saw it, "They had simply closed the door of their lives and vanished from Amsterdam."

✳

"We put on heaps of clothes as if we were going to the north pole."

July 8, 1942

Chapter 3

The Annex

"I'm very afraid that we shall be discovered and be shot," Anne wrote in an early diary entry. But more often than not, her entries were about ordinary, everyday thoughts and activities. For example, the family's first task upon moving into the Annex was to clear old boxes from the former storage area and clean it. Then they had to put away what belongings they were able to bring. Anne and her father took care of these chores.

Miep came to see how they were doing and Anne asked her, "What about Moortje? Have you seen my cat, Moortje?" Anne could not take the animal with her. She also wanted to know if any of her friends had also gone into hiding. Miep went back to check the Frank's apartment but did not see the cat. (Neighbors took him in and gave him a good home.) She also had to tell Anne that she couldn't take the risk of asking about Anne's friends.

Anne, age 10.

(Opposite page)
The Annex, seen from the back, housed Anne and seven others in secrecy.

During the day, a bookcase sat in front of the entrance to the attic in the Annex.

A Safe Haven

The Annex wasn't much of a home, but it would have to do. A bookcase covered the entrance to the stairway leading to it. It was mounted on hinges and swung out of the way, like a door, to permit entry.

There were two small rooms used as bedrooms on the second floor, one for Anne and Margot and the other for their parents. The larger room on the third floor was a kitchen and living room by day. At night, it became Mr. and Mrs. van Daan's bedroom. Their son, Peter, and his cat, Mouschi, who he had managed to bring along, used the other small room on that floor for a bedroom. There was also an attic, where Anne liked to go and read.

Anne made herself at home by hanging pictures of her favorite movie stars on her bedroom wall. She kept up with the latest movie news because Miep kept her supplied with film magazines as they came out.

In November, the Franks took in another Jew who had to hide. He was Dr. Albert Dussel, a dentist they had known. Margot moved in with her parents, and Dr. Dussel shared the other room with Anne.

The crowded conditions and lack of privacy were not the only things making life difficult for those in hiding. The bells in the clock in the nearby church rang every 15 minutes—even at night. Margot and Mrs. Frank hated the sound and had trouble sleeping. The ringing comforted Anne.

During the day, the occupants of the Annex had to walk around in their stocking feet so they wouldn't be heard below in the office. They also couldn't take a chance on someone at work hearing the sound of the toilet flushing upstairs. That had to wait for the evening.

With too many people jammed into too little room, the Franks, the van Daans, and Dr. Dussel had to work hard to get along. They couldn't afford to have arguments. For Anne, this meant "learning to obey, to hold your tongue, to help, to be good, to give in, and I don't know what else."

Anne was not always successful at these tasks. She liked to be "honest" with everyone, saying just what she thought. She wanted people to take her more seriously. The adults, on the other hand, seemed to think that she did almost nothing right. They also didn't care for her temper. At, times her father had to remind her, softly: "self-control." This calmed her.

Having just turned 13, Anne struggled to behave more like a grown-up. Yet some-

At night, the bookcase could swing open to allow the people in the attic a chance to stretch out in the offices below.

✳

"The secret annex is an ideal hiding place. Although it leans to one side and is damp, you'd never find such a comfortable hiding place anywhere in Amsterdam, not even in the whole of Holland."

July 11, 1942

times she doubted whether she wanted to be like the adults she knew. Why, for instance, did they argue "so easily, so much, and over the most idiotic things?"

Always close to her father, Anne dreaded criticism from him because it hurt the most. On the other hand, she felt her mother treated her like a baby. Mrs. Frank seemed unable to understand her younger daughter—or so Anne thought. Anne's mother got depressed easily and tended to see the negative side of things. She found it hard to remain hopeful, given their situation. She thought the war would never end. In this way, she was the opposite of her younger daughter.

Mrs. Frank was always falling short of the ideal mother Anne wanted her to be. Yet Anne could also be honest enough with herself to write: "I wonder if anyone can ever succeed in making their children absolutely content."

Margot was "such a goody-goody, perfection itself," Anne griped. Anne had to admit, however, that she had enough "mischief" for both herself and her sister.

There was little positive that Anne could say about Mrs. van Daan, who felt that Anne was "spoiled." For instance, the "unbearable" woman complained too much when Anne accidentally broke one of her plates. Anne also wrote in her diary that she thought Mrs. van Daan was flirting with her father.

For Mrs. van Daan, it seemed to Anne, no criticism was too petty. She scolded Anne for not eating her vegetables. Once, when Mrs. van Daan did this, Otto Frank pointed out that she hadn't finished her own dinner. That ended the discussion for the evening.

Of the van Daan's son, Peter, Anne wrote in the first few months of hiding that he was "boring," "touchy and lazy," and a "fool." He was also "gawky." It was an opinion she would change greatly over the next few years.

Anne would never feel differently about Dr. Dussel, though. She found him stuffy and preachy. While trying to fall asleep, he sounded like a fish "gasping for breath." She complained that he hogged the bathroom. He lectured her about her bad manners and went "ssh" if he thought she was being too noisy. He had trouble spending time with a teenager who could so quickly change her mind and moods. In her diary, Anne called him "His Lordship."

Still, these eight people, thrown together without first seeing if they could get along,

Dr. Albert Dussel hid with the Franks in the Annex attic.

somehow managed it. They had little choice, since their lives were at stake. Their routine may also have helped. Everything had a fixed time and place in their little world. Outside was the uncertainty of Europe at war and the Nazis who threatened their very lives. Inside was the order: they knew what to expect.

A Strict Routine

Breakfast was at 9:00 A.M., lunch at 1:15 P.M., and dinner at 6 P.M. In the morning, at 8:30, people arrived for work in the office below and stayed until 5:30 P.M. For those nine hours there had to be silence upstairs in the Annex.

Anne usually went to bed at 10:00 P.M. and got up at 7:00 A.M. Although the church bells didn't bother her, Dr. Dussel often did when he came in later to go to sleep. Anne was also awakened sometimes by the sound of the German guns shooting at Allied planes, on their way from England to bomb Germany. If the shooting got too scary, Anne would go into her parent's room, to be comforted by her father.

During the day, Anne read and studied, since she assumed that she would be going back to school after the war. And, of

✻

"I can't tell you how oppressive it is never to be able to go outdoors, I am afraid we shall be discovered and be shot. That is not exactly a pleasant prospect."

July 11, 1942

course, she wrote in her diary. She worked on it either in her room or her parents', when they weren't in it. Anne liked to write when she was alone. The others sometimes teased her about her writing, making her blush.

Miep Gies brought in the food and supplies, so she was often in the Annex. Once, she accidentally came upon Anne at work on her diary in her parents' room. Miep recalls Anne looking up with a "dark" expression. She seemed like another person, not the teenager Miep thought she knew. "It was as if I had interrupted an intimate moment in a very, very private friendship," Miep thought.

At night, Anne could go downstairs into the back rooms of the office, where she and Margot often spent the evening helping with the paperwork for the business. Anne could also peek at the outside world through an opening in the heavy curtains covering the office windows in the front. She might see a dog barking across the canal, which ran alongside the street, and people walking in the rain, carrying umbrellas. Life went on as before. As time went by and the war did not end, she saw that people on the street looked dirtier, less neat and appealing than before.

In May, 1943, Anne watched through the window as British and German planes fought in the skies over Amsterdam. One day in the same year, the war almost came through the roof of the Annex. A British plane was shot down and crashed just a few blocks away. Anne heard it hit the ground.

There were other ways that the outside world seemed to close in on the Annex. As the months dragged on, the war took its toll on the Dutch. There were shortages of everything, including clothing and food. The shortages made things more difficult for Miep Gies. She had to shop for the eight people in hiding, herself, and her husband. She had yet another mouth to feed when the son of a friend went into hiding in her apartment. He had refused to pledge loyalty to Germany. That could have gotten him arrested.

Miep had to shop carefully, making sure nobody noticed that she was buying much more food than she and her husband needed. Luckily, she knew shopkeepers who did not ask too many questions. Even with all her work, by 1943, she was often coming up with little more than "a few beans, some wilted lettuce, half-rotten potatoes."

Life in the Attic Grows Harder

By the time the eight in hiding had been in the Annex for a year, bread and artificial coffee was all they could expect for breakfast. As the food got worse, stomachaches increased. Clothes began to wear out. Shoes no longer fit. The sleeves of Anne's sweaters reached only half-way down her arms. To top it off, Mouschi, Peter's cat, had fleas.

Problems they could have dealt with easily in other times now made life much harder. Anne, for instance, was getting headaches and eyestrain. Miep said she was willing to sneak Anne out of the Annex for a trip to the eye doctor. But Mr. Frank feared it was too dangerous and would not allow it. So Anne put up with the discomfort.

By the summer of 1943, everyone was dreaming of what he or she would do when the war ended. A hot bath in a tub, a real cup of coffee, and going to a movie were some things on their minds. Anne wanted to get back into her own house. She dreamt about walking in the cold fresh air, riding a bike, and dancing. These simple pleasures now seemed far off. They were from a different lifetime.

*

"Our supper today consists of hash made from kale which has been preserved in a barrel....it's incredible how kale can stink when it's a year old. The smell in the room is a mixture of bad plums, strong preservations and rotten eggs."
March 14, 1944

Chapter 4

Hope

Outside, the raids on the Dutch Jews increased. The Nazis would seal off whole neighborhoods, trying to catch every Jew in the area. "Children coming home from school find that their parents have disappeared," Anne wrote in her diary in the beginning of 1943. "Women return from shopping to find their homes shut up and their families gone."

Miep later recalled the horror of the raids. She remembered "the shrill, piercing whistles and then the sounds of boots on steps, rifle butts pounding on doors, insistent ringing of doorbells, and the coarse frightful voice demanding in German, 'Open up! Be quick! Be quick!'" Then the police would herd the sad figures into the street and take them away.

When Dr. Dussel entered the Annex in November 1942, he told those inside that Jews were now going to "a terrible fate."

Anne in May 1941, nearly age 11.

(Opposite page) A young Polish boy raises his hands in terror as Nazis round up Jews in Warsaw, Poland.

Anne felt guilty that she lived in relative comfort while other Jews suffered much worse. Just how much worse became known to those inside through reports from Miep and the other Dutch workers who helped them.

The Nazis, Anne wrote in her diary, treated the Jews "without a shred of decency." As German armies swept quickly through Eastern Europe, they made the Jews who lived there move into small areas called "ghettos." Jews could not leave these places. The most famous of these was the Warsaw ghetto in Poland.

In some areas, special killing units followed the German troops. Once enemy soldiers were cleared out, the special units went to work. They rounded up every Jew they could find, including the elderly, women, and children. These people were often made to dig their own graves—large open pits. Then the Germans led their victims to the edge of the pits and shot them in the back of the head. About 1 million of the 11 million Jews who had lived in Eastern Europe died in this way.

"The Final Solution"

By 1942, the Nazis had decided on a "final solution" to what they viewed as the

"Jewish problem"; they would simply murder every Jew in Europe. When the Nazis found that the method they had been using did not enable them to kill as many people as they wanted to, they developed a more efficient means of mass murder. They shipped their victims to concentration camps. There, Jews were either worked to death or killed in large groups by poison gas. Then their bodies were burned in ovens, the flames suggesting a holocaust.

Many people in the outside world refused to believe that this was actually happening, since the Nazis did not announce what they were doing. At best, those hearing the stories tried not to think about them too much. Otherwise, it might be impossible to carry on anything like a normal life.

Anne was an optimist, but by the fall of 1943, a little more than a year after going into hiding, even she was having trouble finding the bright side of life. One day in September, she realized that she wasn't smiling as much as she used to. Perhaps, she feared, such gloom would make her mouth permanently "droop at the corners." Everyone in the Annex had turned pale from being cooped up. In December, she came down with the flu.

By 1942, the Nazis had constructed concentration camps, designed to imprison and murder Jews. Auschwitz (above), in Poland, was one of the most populated and brutal camps.

It was still hard to get along with the others. The adults Anne lived with seemed to think that teenagers weren't supposed to have their own ideas. They were in hiding and afraid for their lives. Yet, her mother still nagged her to go to bed early and wanted to inspect everything she read.

Sometimes Anne couldn't remember with whom she had recently fought and with whom she was still on good terms. When the walls seemed to close in, she would remind herself how much worse it could be. Then she felt better, and the Annex became "a little piece of blue heaven, surrounded by heavy black rain clouds."

To lighten the sadness, she and her father started writing funny poems to each other. Everyone took advantage of anything special they could celebrate—birthdays, for example. Presents had to be made from whatever was lying around. In the first few months of hiding, for instance, Anne made a special dessert to give as a present. She made it out of sugar she had put aside instead of using it on her breakfast cereal.

Anne also tried to keep her spirits up by looking as good as she could, given the conditions in which they were living. Every night she combed out her brown hair and put it in curlers. She also kept trying out new hair styles and clothing combinations, wondering what she would wear when she went back to school. Miep gave Anne's spirits a big boost one day when she brought her a pair of high heels.

Anne had reached a height of five feet, two inches when she went into hiding. Her awareness of the way her body was changing made her more conscious of how she looked. And Anne looked forward to getting her first period because it seemed "so important."

By the beginning of 1944, Anne was beginning to seem more grown up. She herself realized it. Anne had always had a special ability to see herself as others might look at her. She knew that she had this skill. "I can watch myself and my actions, just like an outsider," she confided to her diary.

Now almost 15, Anne looked back on the year-and-a-half she had spent in the Annex and could see how she was changing. The person she was before she went into hiding had tried to get her way with friends and family by being sweet, cute, and a flirt. That person now seemed "so unreal... amusing, but very superficial."

✳

"The people from whom we obtained food coupons have been caught, so we just have our five ration cards and no extra coupons, and no fats. As both Miep and Koophuis are ill, Elli hasn't time to do any shopping, so the atmosphere is dreary and dejected, and so is the food."

March 14, 1944

Anne felt sad when she looked back at some of the angrier things she had written in her diary about her mother. She realized, though, that at the time she wrote them she had to find a way of letting off steam. Normally, a teenager could go out and work off at least some of those feelings by being active. She couldn't. She was a prisoner—even if, as Miep once pointed out, the door to her "prison" was locked from the inside instead of the outside.

New Interests

As Anne became less a girl and more a young woman, she began to notice other features of the now 17-year-old Peter van Daan besides his "gawkiness." At some point, she became aware of his curly brown hair, and she realized that he wasn't bad company after all. She began to spend more time with him. In the beginning of 1944, she wrote that she had "a queer feeling each time I looked into his deep blue eyes."

Anne and Peter spent a good deal of time together in his room. It was comforting to know that he had some of the same problems with his parents that she had with hers. They talked about everything in a matter-of-fact way, including sex. Anne was

Peter van Daan and his family hid with the Franks in the Annex. As they grew, Peter and Anne became very close friends.

feeling better and better about their growing friendship. That's why she was especially upset that her mother gave her an
odd look one day when Anne came out of
Peter's room. Anne thought it was unfair
for her mother to pry into her life so
closely.

Anne insisted to her diary that she was
not falling in love. But she was soon writing
about "darling Peter," and "Him." When
her father kissed her, she admitted, she
wished it were Peter's lips she was touch-
ing. By February, she was thinking of Peter
all day. In March, she described herself as
"just like someone in love." She even began
to worry that Margot might have some
strong feelings about Peter and could be
jealous. Not so, Margot told her.

Peter told Anne that he liked the way her
dimples looked when she laughed. By
April 1, Anne was no longer trying to deny
her romantic feelings. She wanted Peter to
kiss her. On April 15, he did. Only a few
weeks before, she had wondered if he
thought of her "as a girl or as a sister."
After the kiss, she had something else on
her mind: "Will Peter be content to leave it
at this?"

Anne wasn't sure what she felt or
thought—only that there was a conflict

going on inside her. If they had not been in hiding, if things could have taken a more normal course, if. . . . Yet Peter still seemed a little immature to her, though she had grown deeply fond of him. What should she do?

In doubt, she turned to the one person she always trusted: her father. She told him about the budding romance, but she didn't get the response she had hoped for. He said she should spend less time with Peter. Otto Frank was obviously afraid that the relationship would get out of control.

Anne's response was to write a letter to her father saying that she was old enough to take care of herself. This hurt his feelings, and made her feel even more upset. So just when Anne's world was beginning to brighten, gloom fell on it again.

The passage of time, as it happened, not her father's objections, kept the lid on Anne's romance. Over the next few weeks, she and Peter had good times together. Yet Anne also realized that because of her strange life in hiding, she had an extra strong need to feel close to someone her own age. She needed someone she could talk to as an equal, someone who might understand her. Kitty, her diary, could not always fill that need.

If Anne and Peter had been leading normal lives in the outside world, she would not have let herself get quite so close to him—at least not so quickly. Maybe it would not have been Peter in the first place. Her feelings cooled down just a little, leaving her and Peter with a warm friendship and a touch of romance.

As the summer of 1944 approached, Anne looked to the future. What kind of life would she lead as an adult? She wanted "something besides a husband and children." In addition to the entries in her diary, she wrote stories and sketches to pass the time in hiding. The pleasure she got from writing made her think that she might want to be a journalist someday. The one thing that worried her was that she had already missed two years of school. She wasn't sure if she would want to go back now that she was so far behind the other students.

Volunteers search through the wreckage after German bombs destroyed much of Amsterdam in 1940.

Allied Forces Land in France

Suddenly, there was reason to hope that the war might end soon. On June 6, 1944, (known as "D-Day") news came that American, British, and other Allied forces had landed in France. They were now fighting German soldiers on European soil. Every

On June 6, 1944, Allied forces landed on the beaches of Normandy, France. Known as "D-Day," this landing signaled the final stages of World War II.

day brought news of the progress of the Allies as they pushed steadily toward Germany—and toward the Netherlands. It seemed only a matter of weeks before the Germans would be driven out of Amsterdam. Then eight weary people could leave the Annex and go back to the lives they had left in such a hurry almost two years ago.

Otto Frank marked the progress of the Allies on a map. He stuck pins in it to show how far the soldiers had advanced. The pins steadily moved across the map, day by day. Anne felt that "friends" were coming nearer.

This called for a celebration. As luck would have it, the people in the Annex could now share a special treat. A salesman brought strawberries—a rare treat those days—for the workers in the offices below. Miep took some upstairs and they were able to make jam.

These were days of hope, but also of caution—even fear. Several times over the past two years the Franks and the others hiding with them thought they would be discovered. The first scare came in early 1943, when the building containing the Annex was sold. The new owner might have come upon them, except for the quick thinking of a worker who was helping to keep the hiding place a secret. Showing the new landlord around his property, the worker pretended to have lost the key to the storage area. Fortunately, the new owner never asked about it again.

Several times, the residents of the Annex thought they heard burglars breaking into the downstairs office at night. Sometimes it was just the wind; once it was rats running across the floor. They feared not that thieves might take something but that they would find their hiding place. Perhaps they would see something unusual and guess what was going on. Once, for example, the occupants of the Annex remembered that they had left their chairs gathered around the office radio, which they sometimes listened to at night. Might thieves figure out that people were in hiding there and tell the police? Nothing happened.

✳

"Could we be granted victory this year, 1944? We don't know yet, but hope is revived within us: it gives us fresh courage, and makes us strong again."
June 6, 1944

Their fears were reasonable. The Nazis rewarded anyone who turned in Jews. They would not care if they had to pay off common criminals for leading them to a Jew in hiding. As Miep later described the situation, in those days "a thief was safe and a Jew was not."

At Easter, thieves did break in. Would the police come and poke around, perhaps finding the place where eight Jews were hiding? They did come to look, but fortunately they were not curious enough to search every inch of the building. Anne and the others could take no chances. They remained silent for two days over the holiday, putting up with extreme discomfort to make sure that they were not found out. It was a reminder of just how shaky their position was.

Every Jew in hiding had to worry about being found by accident, as almost happened to the Franks. Even more disturbing was the chance that betrayal could put them in the hands of the Nazis. For some Jews in the Netherlands, danger was now coming from people they trusted. Many Dutch who had helped to hide them were having second thoughts about the chance they were taking.

With food and every other necessity hard to find, the Nazis' reward for turning in Jews was tempting. Anti-Semitism was on the rise, as more people began to blame the Jews for their hardships.

Some Dutch were also getting tired of endangering their own lives by helping Jews to escape the Nazis. The man who had been supplying Miep with vegetables for those in hiding was arrested for hiding Jews himself. People heard about incidents like this one and some began to wonder if it was worth the continued risk. All it took was a phone call to the gestapo to take the "problem" off their hands.

Of the 25,000 Jews in the Netherlands who tried to survive the war by hiding, the Nazis discovered 9,000. They were taken away to concentration camps. Many of these thousands were arrested because someone turned them in.

With good news one day, bad the next, and fear an almost constant companion, it's amazing that Anne could remain hopeful most of the time. It would have been easy for her to become bitter about how the world had treated her and other Jews. Yet, in July she wrote in her diary that she still believed people were "good at heart."

Chapter 5

In the Shadow of Death

Anne in May, 1942, almost age 13.

Anne's belief in the goodness of people was tested on the morning of August 4, 1944. It was Friday. Miep was working in the office downstairs. She looked up from her desk and saw a man standing in the doorway. He was husky, middle-aged, about average height, and wearing civilian clothing. He was also pointing a gun at her. "Don't move," he said. He spoke with an Austrian accent. She could hear several more men entering other parts of the office and going up the stairs into the Annex. They seemed to know about the shelves that covered the secret entrance to the hiding place.

Otto Frank was giving Peter van Daan an English lesson when he heard the footsteps on the stairs. There was no time to run. Besides, there would have been nowhere to run to. The Dutch Nazi policemen who came into the hiding place rounded up the eight Jews and gave them five minutes to pack a few belongings. Each filled the little knapsack they had kept ready for a quick escape from a fire or other danger in the Annex.

Anne had stored her diary—by then filling several notebooks and loose pieces of paper—in her father's briefcase. One of the arresting policeman asked Otto Frank if he had any jewelry. Mr. Frank said he did not but there was some silverware. The officer picked up the briefcase and emptied it onto the floor so that he might use it to carry away the silverware. The papers that fell out when he emptied the briefcase did not interest him. He left Anne's diary scattered on the floor.

Anne could have gathered up the papers and taken them, but for some reason she didn't. Perhaps she simply had more important things on her mind, such as what would happen to them now.

The Gestapo officer who led the arrest team, the one with the Austrian accent, began talking to Otto Frank. He was impressed that Anne's father had served in the German army in World War I. Nevertheless, the Nazi did what he had come to do. Each of the eight Jews was led downstairs at gunpoint. It was all done quietly.

*

On August 1, 1944 Anne writes in her diary for the last time.

No one cried. They were put into a green police truck, which drove up the street, crossed over the canal, made a turn, and sped off to the police station.

It was all over by noon. Later, Miep and another woman who had helped the Franks while they were in hiding went upstairs. The Annex was now deserted, except for Mouschi, Peter's cat. They found the diary on the floor and took it. Miep promised to hold it for Anne "until she comes back."

After being questioned at the police station, the Franks, the van Daans, and Dr. Dussel were taken to a Dutch prison called Westerbork. They traveled to the prison on a regular passenger train, as if they were just going on a trip. Anne spent much of the time gazing out the window at the scenery.

A Brief Stay at Westerbork

At Westerbork, the Frank family was able to stay together, making their time almost "pleasant," according to Otto Frank. Anne and Peter spent a good deal of time with each other. One person who saw them there said they looked "happy." Added to the enjoyment of each other's company was the hopeful thought—not unrealistic—that the war might end soon, or at least the Allied troops might reach Westerbork and free them.

Their hopes ended in early September. One day, the Nazis told the prisoners to get ready to be moved. That could mean only one thing: they were being sent to a concentration camp. It was to be the last shipment of prisoners from Westerbork to the camps. If they had been arrested a few weeks later, they would have been safe.

Throughout Westerbork, parents made children memorize the address of places at which they could meet their families after the war if they were separated—and if they lived. The beginning of their trip did not encourage them to believe in that possibility. The Jews were herded into freight cars like cattle. There were 75 people in each car—barely enough room in which to stand—with only one small window for fresh air.

After they had traveled for days like this, the train suddenly stopped. They had arrived at Auschwitz, a concentration camp in Poland. As the doors slid open, the prisoners stared into bright lights at German guards, who had attack dogs as well as guns. The women prisoners were told they would have to march for an hour to the special women's camp called Birkenau. Small children and those who were too old or ill to walk were told to get on buses. Those who got on were taken directly to the gas chambers and immediately killed.

The others were put in barracks, where they were given barely enough food to keep them alive and hardly enough clothing to keep them warm in the cold Polish winter. Thousands died of disease or froze to death. Those who didn't, were worked and beaten until many of them dropped. When the prisoners grew too weak to work, they too were gassed to death and their bodies burned.

Women and children in rags were crowded together and starved at the Bergen-Belsen concentration camp.

From the few people who saw Anne during this time—and lived to tell about it— we know that she faced this horror with as much courage as anyone could. At Birkenau her head was shaved, like all the other prisoners. For clothing, she wore a gray sack. Anne was somehow able to keep her humanity. She could still cry when she saw the German guards lead children away to be gassed.

A Family Torn Apart

In October 1944, Anne and Margot were separated from their mother and sent to another camp, called Bergen-Belsen. If anything, living conditions there were even worse and food more scarce. A friend of Anne's from before the war saw her there and spoke to her through the barbed wire that separated different parts of the camp. When they recognized each other, the two old friends wept. By this time, Anne was wearing rags and had become very thin. Only Anne's eyes still seemed to express her personality.

Typhus, a deadly disease, now swept through the barracks of weakened and starving prisoners. Margot died first. One day she became unconscious and fell off the wooden platform on which she slept. When people nearby tried to pull her back, they realized that she was dead. They did not tell Anne, who was herself already gravely ill. A few days later, in March 1945, just a few weeks before the war in Europe would end, Anne died. She was 15 years old.

After her daughters were taken away, Edith Frank slowly lost her mind and her will to live. She died at Birkenau in January 1945. Dr. Dussel died in the concentration camp, as did Mr. and Mrs. van Daan. Peter was taken away by the Germans as the war neared its end. Needing more workers, they marched him from Poland to Germany. The strain was too much, and it killed him.

Of the eight who hid for two years in the Annex, only Otto Frank lived through the war. He managed to stay alive at Auschwitz. There he ran into a friend of Anne's. She remembered him looking like a skeleton. "Is Anne with you?" he asked. "Have you seen her or Margot?" The girl had not.

Eventually, the Russian army reached Auschwitz, freeing the prisoners. They were taken by train to Russia. It was on the trip to Russia that Otto learned that his wife had died.

Hitler Is Defeated

The Germans surrendered in the spring of 1945. Gradually, Jews began to return to the Netherlands. Of the 60,000 Dutch Jews shipped to Auschwitz, only a little over a thousand were still alive.

Otto Frank came back to Amsterdam— and to his old office beneath the Annex. Miep Gies invited him to live with her and her husband in their house, and he accepted the offer.

Otto still held out hope that somehow his daughters had survived. He had heard nothing about them. Then, six weeks after the war ended, he received a letter from

someone who gave him the news he dreaded. They would never return.

Miep Gies could not bring herself to read Anne's diary until a year or two after the war. When she finally did, she felt that

Diseased and starving, these inmates of the Buchenwald concentration camp were used as slave labor until they died or were murdered by Nazis.

A movie about Anne Frank's life was made in 1957. It was based on a Broadway play from 1955, which gained wide acclaim.

"now Anne's voice would never be lost." Otto told friends about the diary. It revealed a person more complicated than the daughter he thought he knew. Many people urged him to have it published. At first he resisted, but then gave in. Several Dutch publishers turned it down, but finally one accepted it.

Gradually, the diary's fame spread, and it was translated into many languages. It was even translated into German, although Otto first toned down some parts in which Anne was very critical of the Germans.

A play based on the diary was produced in 1955 and won the Pulitzer Prize for drama. When it opened in Germany, in 1956, it was sometimes greeted with loud applause, at other times with silence. A German newspaper wrote that the silence might have been caused by the audience's "shame" that Germans had done such terrible things. Students have often performed the play. A high school boy who had acted in a production of it once wrote to Otto Frank to tell him how much it had moved him. He felt that the play had made him lose whatever prejudice he may have had toward people who were different from himself. He realized that "not only does Anne stand for the Jews, but for any human being who suffered because of his beliefs, colour or race."

The play was turned into a movie in 1957. Also in that year, the Anne Frank Foundation was set up to care for the Annex, which became a museum. Every year, about half a million people visit the place where Anne Frank and seven other Jews hid from the Nazis.

Some people were never moved by the tragedy of the Holocaust. There are those who refuse to believe that it happened. After the war, many Nazis claimed to have no responsibility for it—even those who actually did the killing. They said that they were just following orders.

In 1963, the gestapo agent who had led the raid on the Annex was found. He was working as a policeman in Austria and was suspended from his job without pay. When interviewed by a reporter, he said, "Why pick on me after all these years? I only did my duty." Then he complained that he had just bought some furniture and would have trouble paying for it without his salary. Had he read Anne's diary? he was asked. He had, recently, but only to see if he was in it. (Anne's last entry came before the arrest, so he wasn't.) After a year's suspension, he was back on the police force.

The former gestapo man could shed no light on a question that many people wanted answered. Who had betrayed the people in the Annex? Who told about their hiding place? He couldn't remember. "There were so many betrayals during those years," he explained.

Otto Frank was not one of those anxious to have the answer to that question. "I don't want to know who did it," he said. He moved to Switzerland in 1952. In 1953, he married a woman who had also survived a concentration camp. He died in 1980.

Otto Frank's second wife had lost all of her family in the Holocaust except her daughter, a girl Anne's age, who had known Anne before the war. That girl recently wrote about how she felt when she was freed from the camp in which she was held. "I was a teenager who had survived the tragedy of Auschwitz and I supposed I would be going back to normal life, back to school with teachers and schoolfriends, doing everyday things which for many years had been forbidden and out of reach to me. Suddenly I felt very scared."

What if Anne had survived? What would life have been like for her? What might she have done as an adult? We will never know. Yet, as Miep Gies pointed out, Anne's voice

Otto Frank, shown here at age 90, was the only member of the Annex group to survive the war. He died in 1980.

Anne Frank's diary continues to touch people around the world and remind them of a time and place that should never be forgotten.

lives. It has spoken to the millions who have read her diary or seen the play or the movie. Anne was just an ordinary 13-year-old girl who faced the darkness with as much courage and optimism as she could. She also set an example for everyone, everywhere.

At one place in her diary, Anne wrote that "everything is so different from ordinary times and from ordinary people's lives. What can a person do in the face of such evil?"

There is perhaps only one answer: they can remember the Holocaust so it won't happen again—to Jews or to anyone else. Anne helps us to remember. She brought the Holocaust down to a human level. As Judith Miller, a journalist, has put it, "We must remind ourselves that the Holocaust was not 6 million. It was one, plus one, plus one. . ." It happened not to numbers, but to individual men, women, and children, like Anne Frank.

Glossary

Explaining New Words

Allies The countries, including the United States, that fought Germany, Italy, and Japan in World War II.

anti-Semitism Anti-Jewish prejudice.

concentration camps Nazi prisons where Jews and others were used as slave labor, tortured, and killed.

Crystal Night Rioting in Germany, November 9, 1938, when Jewish property was destroyed and many Jews were killed.

final solution The Nazi plan to kill all the Jews in Europe.

gestapo The Nazi secret police.

Adolf Hitler Nazi leader, dictator of Germany, who ordered the murder of 6 million Jews.

Holocaust A great fire in which victims are sacrificed. It has come to symbolize the murder of 6 million Jews.

Nazis The political party, started in Germany, based on hate, prejudice, and rule by threat of violence.

storm troopers Nazi party members used to intimidate people through the threat of violence.

For Further Reading

Anne Frank Foundation. *Anne Frank in the World*. Amsterdam: Anne Frank Foundation, 1985.

Barnouw, David, and Gerrold van der Stroom, eds. *The Diary of Anne Frank: The Critical Edition*. Arnold J. Pomerans and B. M. Mooyaart-Doubleday, trans. New York: Doubleday, 1989.

Eisenberg, Azriel. *The Lost Generation: Children in the Holocaust*. New York: Pilgrim Press, 1982.

Gies, Miep with Alison Leslie Gold. *Anne Frank Remembered: The Story of the Woman Who Helped to Hide the Frank Family*. New York: Simon & Schuster, 1987.

Miller, Judith. *One, by One, by One: Facing the Holocaust.* New York: Simon & Schuster, 1990.

Rittner, Carol, and Sondra Myers, eds. *The Courage to Care: Rescuers of Jews During the Holocaust.* New York: New York University Press, 1986.

Schloss, Evan, with Evelyn Julia Kent. *Eva's Story: A Survivor's Tale by the Step-sister of Anne Frank.* New York: St. Martin's Press, 1988.

Schnabel, Ernest. *Anne Frank: A Portrait in Courage.* Richard and Clara Winston, trans. New York: Harcourt, Brace & World, 1958.

Steenmeijer, Anna G., ed., in collaboration with Otto Frank and Henri van Praag. *A Tribute to Anne Frank.* Garden City, N.Y.: Doubleday, 1971.

Index

Photo credits:

Cover: Anne Frank Stichting, Amsterdam; pps. 4, 5, 7, 8, 9, 12,
13, 14, 20, 22, 24, 25, 26, 27, 29, 35, 40, 48: © Anne Frank
Stichting, Amsterdam; pps. 6, 16, 17, 18, 34, 59: AP/Wide World
Photos; pps. 10, 11, 19, 21, 37, 43, 44, 52, 55, 58: UPI/Bettmann;
p. 56: Photofest.

Photo research: Ellen Cibula